Old LOSSIEMOUTH

by

Donald Stewart

Until 1945, the horse and cart was still a major part of the transport system of Lossie, and Millar Alexander is about to take his daughter Margaret and her friends on a very important journey – to the annual Sunday School Picnic. The horse has been fed and watered, Millar has changed into his suit, soon the benches will be put on the cart and then – off to the country for a day of fun and games, followed by tea and buns. It may have been only two miles from home, but it felt like a journey into space. The horse, Kate, had rejected the country as her permanent home a few years earlier. Millar had decided to replace her and part-exchanged her to a farmer ten miles inland. As soon as the new owner had fed her and left her in her new quarters, she kicked down the stable door and set out for home, following the route used to deliver her. She was seen in the sma' 'oors plodding along through Elgin and Bishopmill. On reaching home at 6 a.m., she kicked down the door of her old stable, and was found later munching the hay in her own stall where she spent the rest of her days.

ISBN 9781840330892

Printed by P2D, 17 Burgess Road, Hastings, TN35 4NR

ACKNOWLEDGEMENTS

Many people helped in the collecting of the photographs used in this book. Without their help it would never have been completed.

The picture on page 6 is reproduced by permission of Aerofilms Ltd. (telephone 0208 207 0666). The picture on page 48 is reproduced courtesy of Robert Grieves.

The publishers regret that they cannot supply copies of any pictures featured in this book.

Carries in Queen Street was probably the smartest and best run shop of its day. Assistants with white aprons hurried to fetch items wanted by the customer, weighing, parcelling, and finally tying with string, stout paper bags of sugar, flour etc. The racks of biscuit boxes were immaculately filled, and hidden behind the counter was the small boy's favourite – broken biscuits sold by the pennyworth. The brass-encrusted till may have been specially featured to remind customers that this was 'A Cash and Carry Store'.

INTRODUCTION

At the end of the last millennium (AD 1000), the mouth of the River Lossie was situated somewhere near Kirkhill, three miles inland from its present position. The Coulard Hill was probably an island, with the Fort and Cathedral of Kinneddar at its south-west tip near the Coulardbank Hotel. Ships could sail right up to the Bishop's Palace at Spynie, carrying cargo for Elgin merchants. Around the twelfth century, the passages at Roseisle and Kinneddar became blocked, leaving a long sea loch from Spey Bay past the castle at Duffus, although the passage was much shallower than before. About AD 1500, this passage became completely blocked as successive storms drove banks of stones into the gap, and Spynie was cut off from the sea and thus from shipping. Three of the stony ridges can still be clearly seen at the Seatown Caravan Park. The bank ends at Sunbank Farm where the depth of the stones is also visible in the nearby excavations.

Present day Lossiemouth – Lossie to the locals – formed over the past 250 years as three distinct areas developed and grew into each other. The oldest part, the village of Stotfield on the north side of the Coulard Hill, was home to a small number of fishing families who operated out of the Hythe (now used by the local sailing club). They endured a dreadful disaster on Christmas Day 1806. All 21 able bodied men set out in three boats on a fine morning, but vanished without trace when a storm broke, drowning 10 Edwards, 4 Youngs, 3 McLeods, a Mitchell, a Baikie, a Crockett, and a Main newly arrived from Nairn. They left 17 widows, 47 children and 8 aged parents, who were saved from destitution by an appeal fund which raised £1,152, providing support until 1842.

At the other end of the town, the two boats which worked the river mouth didn't go to sea that day, and survived. The river mouth had been developed by the Elgin magistrates a number of years earlier (the date 1629 is carved on one of the buildings), to replace the cargo facilities lost when Spynie became landlocked. A new town with streets forty-two feet wide and lanes of twenty-one feet developed from the cliff face southwards, to service the new port.

As Scotland began to prosper, so did the fishing boats, and as herring fishing, curing and marketing became the norm, replacing the local selling of line-caught cod and haddock, fishing grew into a sizeable industry. Alas, the river port was never a great success, with its difficult entrance only open for a short time at each tide. In 1839 the Laird of Pitgaveny had the vision to see that a better port could be made by cutting into the deserted rocky headland known as Stotfield Point, and created the basin of the present harbour for cargo boats to use. This soon proved so successful that the square basin was extended south to where the new Morayshire Railway built its terminus in 1852, with lines running along the quays for goods traffic. Fishing boats also used the harbour and their increasing number resulted in the development of a second basin to the west. Fisher families flocked to the harbour, building houses in Lossie's second planned new town of

Branderburgh, named after the Laird. The population doubled between 1851 and 1881. Most of the newcomers came from the fishing villages between Buckie and Portknockie, towards which the new harbour pointed.

The Seatown, an enclave of 51 houses trapped between the river and the canal which drained the Loch of Spynie, was always inhabited by fishermen, and at one stage 31 of the families were Stewarts because their early families consisted almost entirely of boys. One girl was known throughout her long life as Dother (daughter) as she was the only girl among many brothers. The Seatown men beached their boats on the river bank and did not use the new harbour for many years, so that the bridge over the river, built in 1911, had an opening centre section to allow the passage of the boats. A few keels lying on the river bed are all that remain of this once busy area.

At the turn of the century steam displaced sail as the means of powering the herring boats, and the fleet changed completely from one type of vessel to the other within a decade. The sailboats had already started sailing to the East Anglian fishing, and local girls, known as quines, followed them to gut the herring and pack them into barrels. 90% of the output was exported to Germany and Russia, but this trade stopped completely in 1914 as we fought one customer and couldn't reach the other. With both overseas customers bankrupt after the war, a series of disastrous seasons convinced the Lossie men that a new way of life was needed, and they tried a method of fishing they had seen the Danes using. The seine net was to be their salvation, and after John Campbell launched the *Marigold*, the first custom-built seine-netter, the fleet once again changed type completely within a decade. So successful were the seine-netters that Lossie soon became Scotland's premier white fish port.

The original Lossiemouth, often called Old Lossie or, by the fishers, the Country Town, became associated with farm or building workers and consisted of narrow feus, long enough to keep hens or grow vegetables on. It grew outwards with time, and every feu has now been subdivided with another house built on it. Meanwhile Branderburgh steadily climbed the hill, and calling a house Whinnybank or Rockyknowe was a description of its position, not just whimsy! Stotfield and Branderburgh met when the Big Greenie, used for drying herring nets, became the Marine Park in 1935. Coulard Hill is now completely covered as the council and Ministry of Defence have filled the space between the Elgin Road and Stotfield with housing schemes containing the town's only supermarket.

Today, the small number of fishermen who still live in the town sail from Peterhead to fish in Norwegian waters, or from Lochinver to fish the new frontier on the Atlantic Shelf, and are not allowed to land in Lossie as it is not 'designated'. Most townsfolk now work in Elgin, or in the aerodrome built at the start of World War II.

After a few early floods, the residents of the Seatown successfully strengthened and raised the river bank to its present level. This flood was caused by a cloudburst, and the children are enjoying the fun. The dog would have been less happy a century earlier, as he would probably have been killed and his skin used to make a buoy for use at sea. This practice earned the locals the name Dogwallers, which they have been known as ever since.

The early fishing was done with lines and hooks using mussels as bait for the cod and haddock. This picture shows Alexander Thomson, known as Sandy 'Caukie' because he was one of the small number of Catholics in the town, disentangling his lines prior to baiting the hooks. Mussels, brought across the Moray Firth from Tain, were stored at the riverbank until needed. Present-day gardeners may well be puzzled when they find fragments of blue shells as they dig, but these were simply left behind when the women and old men baited the hooks.

Lossiemouth Fisherman at his Lines.

Like the river port, the new harbour was built to provide cargo facilities, and this photograph shows it filled with half a dozen barques and several brigs in 1882. The large building on the left was the Bank of Scotland, well situated to watch over its investments.

Designing a harbour is a complex task, since vessels must be able to enter it, and then be protected when the are moored. This picture shows the North pier deflecting most of the wave energy away from the harbour, while the waves that are allowed to enter are expended on the spending beach. The solid rock from which the harbour was cut can be seen outside the walls; stones removed after the collapse of the North pier in 1936 lie to the right. At low water, the rock can be seen below the masonry level. Since the photograph was taken the railway has been removed, along with the oil tanks. The three slips have been dismantled and Dunn's sheds, full of noise and smoke in the past, lie abandoned.

Pansy (INS 1305)

In the nineteenth century there were two principal types of fishing boat. Scaffies had a steeply raked bow and stern, while those of fifies were almost vertical. When William Campbell 'Dad' (right) wanted a new boat built he chose a vertical bow and a steeply raked stern. The decision followed much heart-searching, and extensive discussion with his wife, and the result was the *Nonsuch* (INS 2118), launched in 1878 from William Wood's yard in Lossie. The heart-searching was shared by the local boat-builders, and Wood brought two men up from Fife to make sure they got it right. The *Nonsuch* proved to be vastly superior in handling and speed to either of the previous designs and became known as the Zulu, after the wars being fought at the time. The *Pansy* (INS 1305) was built soon after, and shows the spread of sail these boats could carry. The design was to last until the sailboat became obsolete with the advent of steam drifters.

The first boat to be constructed specifically for seine net fishing was the *Marigold* (INS 234), owned by John Campbell 'Huntly' (above), nephew of William Campbell. With her 36 hp Gardner engine and crew of 4, her running costs were much lower than those of the steam drifters, and she soon recouped her cost with steady landings of cod, haddock and whiting in the various seasons. Typically a drifter using seine nets cost £20-£25 per week to run as opposed to £10 for the *Marigold*. A loan from the bank was withdrawn just as the *Marigold* was about to be built, and Huntly's cousin, John West, a fish curer, provided the necessary funds.

Lossiemouth from Harbour

At the end of the nineteenth century the harbour was a very busy place, and this picture shows it with a large pile of barrels awaiting collection for the herring fishing season. The logs in the foreground were probably destined to become pit props for the rapidly expanding coal mines in the south. Steamers such as the one on the right (probably discharging coal or cement), spelled the eventual demise of the sailing vessels. The sea wall on the left has clearly been patched and was to be almost completely destroyed in the 1936-37 storms.

As the number and size of the fishing boats increased, their presence in what had been conceived and built as a cargo landing facility became a problem, and in 1857 the Harbour Company built the West Basin, usually referred to as the New Harbour, with a bridge – the Briggie – across its entrance. This was soon found to be superfluous and the landward portion removed. The other half survived into the 1940s when the rocky area on the right was concreted over to prevent damage to the boats as they entered and left the basin. A side effect of this was that more wave energy was allowed to enter the basin, causing some boats to break their moorings in stormy weather.

Larger steamships with deeper draughts meant that the harbour had to be deepened, and this picture shows the work in progress in 1892. The building just visible on the left was the first in Branderburgh, built as a residence for the Laird, and now, with a second storey added, the Brander Arms public house. Next to it is the original lifeboat shed, rendered useless following the construction of the West Basin. Other buildings on the left were probably for fish processing and have since been removed.

Launch of the Lifeboat, Lossiemouth.

Lossiemouth's first lifeboat station was established in 1859, and a lifeboat was maintained until 1923 when it was removed to Buckie. The shed at the west end of the new harbour was built to replace the original one in 1899. A purpose-built slipway allowed faster launches, but on stormy days it became impossible for the lifeboat to leave the basin because of the number of fishing boats tied up in the harbour. This picture shows the *James Finlayson* on her inaugural launch in 1905. She was built at a cost of £1,245 to replace the *Frances Sprot*, but was only called out four times before her departure. William Stewart was coxswain from 1893 to 1918, then George McLeod until 1923. The new boat, named by Mrs Thorne of Dunconusg, was handed over to the RNLI by Provost Peterkin, who had just returned from turning on the town's new water supply. The party enjoyed a grand meal in the town hall afterwards.

Lossiemouth from West Harbour.

Without the spire of St James's Church on the skyline it would be difficult today to recognise this as a view of Shore Street and Kinneddar Street, so used have we become to the black corrugated iron sheds of John Dunn and Co. which now occupy the space in the centre of the picture. Several sets of 'steppies' used to provide access to the quayside from Shore Street. Just visible above the dyke is the top of one of the cast iron water supply outlets, or 'pumpies', from which people collected their water by the bucketful. Previously supplies were delivered by Water Willie McDonald's cart at a halfpenny per bucket.

12

The quines provided the labour force for the gutting of the herring and always managed a smile for the camera, although their backs would be breaking, their feet freezing and their fingers stinging from cuts and the brine in which the herring lay. Still, they were away from home and even if their huts were totally without amenities, the camaraderie, and the chance to see their lads at church or at the very popular Revivalist meetings on Sundays, carried them through the long, hard weeks.

Although life at the gutting was hard, the quines still managed to enjoy themselves. This picture shows Jane Mitchell, Teenie Scott and Janet Stewart (seated), and Teenie Smith, Helen Stewart and Annie Edwards (standing). Having just collected their pay, the girls decided to be photographed in their new dresses, which in the case of Janet Stewart became her wedding dress soon after her return home. Helen and Janet were sisters, and their brother Jimmie and their husbands combined with a young engineer to have the *Briar* (INS 420) built in 1928. This was a typical example of how families worked together, and the system worked well unless a boat was lost, when an entire family could be driven to destitution simultaneously.

THE BLOCKED ENTRANCE TO LOSSIEMOUTH HARBOUR
AFTER COLLAPSE OF NORTH PIER DURING STORM, 19TH FEBRUARY 1936

Because of the actions of the waves, tide and river, which all vary and often conflict, entering Lossie harbour has always required an element of luck as well as skill, and many boats have been pushed sideways into the rocky hole at the South pier. This was named the Maggie Duncan Hole after the first boat to be wrecked there, although fortunately not a single life was ever lost in the hole. A couple of days after this 1933 photograph of the *Branderburgh* was taken, a storm blew up wrecking her completely. Her skipper, Jocky Flett, had observed at the end of her first season in 1911 that everything needed money spent on it except the wheel-house windows, and declared that his next boat would be made of glass! The old North pier seems already to have had a new point, and the later break (inset) was at or near the point behind the group of onlookers where a distinct change in colour in the masonry is visible.

The stone blocks used to make the original North pier had been floated along the coast from the Clashach Quarry near Hopeman. On the night of 19 February 1936 they proved unable to withstand a terrible storm and were washed into the harbour mouth. Fortunately the fishing fleet had been almost entirely driven into Burghead or Buckie harbours as the storm developed, and only eight boats were trapped. The stones were painstakingly cleared, but without the protection of the North pier the less substantial South sea wall took such a battering in the next severe storm that the sea almost broke through into the original basin. Both damaged areas were replaced with monolithic reinforced concrete structures, and some of the damaged stones dumped over the North sea wall where they remain today.

Young Joseph Campbell is learning about fishing literally at his grandfather's knee, as the old men discuss the latest changes in boats and fishing, probably disapprovingly. John Campbell favours the skipper's peaked cap, Joe Campbell has a woollen scarf, while George Stewart (Stainies) wears the tweed cap worn by most fishermen. Sadly he was the first father to be bereaved in the 1939 war, as his daughter Annie Bella was lost when the SS *Athenia* was torpedoed by a U-boat in the Atlantic eight hours after war had been declared. Young Joe went on to serve his time as a shipwright in Slater's yard, becoming a fisherman when it closed.

FISH MARKET, LOSSIEMOUTH

From about 3 p.m. boats began to land their catches ready for them to be auctioned and processed before dispatch to Glasgow or Billingsgate by lorry or train. The onlookers are probably visitors, as local women would never have ventured onto the market. The *Maggie Cowie* (INS 78), is typical of the first phase of motorboat design, which was really a copy of the earlier sailboats. The *Devotion* (INS 223) shows how the newer boats had lengthened, and has the rounded cruiser stern which gave the crew more working space.

THE HARVEST OF THE SEA, LOSSIEMOUTH.

A.1238

The fish were lined up for auction, with cod sold by the score and smaller fish by the box. Before the advent of the seine-net, catches of white fish had been much smaller, and auctions on this much larger scale required the construction of a covered market. Herring were sold largely by contract between the crew and a fish-curer, a deal being struck before they were caught.

When Prince Charles enrolled at Gordonstoun School, 3 miles to the west of Lossie, the Queen became a regular visitor, in this case arriving on board the Royal Yacht *Britannia* and landing to the cheers of the local population in the Royal Barge.

For all of its working life, the river port had an entrance consisting of piles of rocks defining its banks, as this view, embellished with a flock of birds shows. The present concrete walls date from 1915, by which time the river was scarcely used. The Station Hotel, opened in 1854, with its 'six bedrooms, a parlour and two water closets' is the imposing building on the left, with stables (later a garage) on one side, and the stationmaster's house on the other. The single storey sandstone station with part-sheltered platform replaced the original wooden building in 1890. The sea wall belonging to the railway company was a relatively thin affair and fresh pointing can be seen, suggesting early wave damage. The old North pier is visible behind the marker post.

It had always been women's work to sell the fish caught by their men, and the arrival of the railway allowed them to extend their range. This group, Maggie Main, Annie Crockett, Maggie Scott and Mary Ralph (women were usually referred to by their maiden names) would travel to regular customers in Elgin, or even as far as Aberlour. Others walked out to farms and some to Calcots or Urquhart, selling to the 'big hooses', and bartering at the farms, which meant carrying the creels back full of vegetables and eggs. They would also be on the lookout for sawdust and wood chippings for their fish-smoking activities.

The town hall was opened in 1885 with a procession which appears to have been made up entirely of Branderburgh residents. It was several years before the library and burgh chambers was added on the right, and the outline of the side windows, which were filled in at the time, is still visible inside the hall. A clock costing £100 was given to the town by the Laird and placed on the left-hand tower. It had originally been intended for a lower turret specially built above the library entrance, but it was realised that this would have made it much less visible. An early regulation forbade the use of the hall for dancing on the grounds that it encouraged 'a tendency to immoral conduct', but this was rescinded and the hall is remembered for the rowdy dances of the 1939-45 war which earned it the nickname of 'Stalingrad'.

At the turn of the century sailboats were still tying up at the Seatown, and the bridge over the river had yet to be built. The large house on the left was built as a dower house for the Gordons of Gordonstoun, and the low buildings adjoining it must have been the stables. These were later turned into a garage, and more recently the houses and shops were demolished to make an extended forecourt. The ruin opposite was demolished to make way for the 'Electric Station' (see page 47).

RAMSAY MACDONALD

Lossie's most famous son was born James MacDonald Ramsay in 1866 in a small cottage beside the railway line, his mother Annie Ramsay having refused to marry his father, James MacDonald. He was always known as James Ramsay MacDonald, but in later years the Tory press said that he had changed his name to hide his illegitimacy, as if such a thing was possible in a small town!

Ramsay first attended the Free Kirk school in the town, where he was mercilessly thrashed by a teacher who had thrashed the young James Barrie in a previous employment. The teacher drowned a couple of years later. Ramsay subsequently went to the parish school at Drainie, two miles walk each way, where the dominie, James Macdonald, plus a sewing mistress and a pupil-teacher, taught seventy pupils in the two classrooms. Macdonald told the pupils: 'You must master: that is education: when you have mastered one thing, you are well on the way to master all things'. Ramsay was a pupil for ten years before being promoted to pupil-teacher, starting a cricket club and later the Lossiemouth Field Club, where he presented various papers including a 44 page treatise on the geological structure of the Coulard Hill.

In 1885 Ramsay made an unsuccessful foray to Bristol, but left in 1886 for London, arriving shortly before a severe economic depression. His first job involved addressing envelopes for ten shillings a week. An active socialist by this time, he became secretary to a Liberal MP at the princely salary of £100 a year. He soon became a successful journalist, a London councillor and secretary of the embryonic Labour Party. His journalism took him to the Boer War where he was absolutely horrified by the conditions in which the British army kept Boer families in their concentration camps. This was to lead him to be a pacifist when the Great War broke out in 1914. He resigned from the chairmanship of the Labour Party when it voted to support the declaration of war, which had been opposed by several Cabinet Ministers, and joined a first-aid corps on the Western Front. He was drummed out of the Moray Golf Club, whose members mainly consisted of Edinburgh and London lawyers and businessmen, for his beliefs, and the word traitor was daubed on the house he had built in Lossie – the Hillocks.

After the war he returned to politics and soon became leader of the Labour Party, by now fighting under its own name instead of via the Liberal Party. In 1924 he became the first Socialist Prime Minister, but he was head of a minority government, and the country was in the middle of a financial crisis which was to dominate his premiership. He attempted a rapprochement with Russia, including restarting the trade in cured herrings which had been the mainstay of North-east fishermen, and this may have created the conditions which led to the infamous Zinovief letter. Now accepted as a forgery concocted by Russian émigrés, but willingly seized upon by the *Daily Mail* and the secret services, this appeared to agree to the Soviet Union taking over the running of Britain. It was published a week before the General Election at which Ramsay was attempting to gain a majority. He lost, but was returned in 1929 with a government again facing a huge financial crisis. This engulfed the country and most of the western world in 1931.

Ramsay wanted to resign but was told by the King that this was tantamount to desertion, and he agreed to form a coalition government. This was seen as treachery by most of his party, and he was expelled, never to rejoin, being vilified for the second time in his life as a traitor, but this time to the Labour Party. He retired as premier in 1935. In 1937, a tired and broken man, he attended the funeral of his friend Sir James Barrie, and sailed for South America on the *Reina del Pacifico* soon after. He died at sea, and his body was returned on the cruiser HMS *Apollo* to be cremated in London. Ramsay's ashes were taken by train to Lossie, where they were met by the Glasgow Orpheus Choir before being taken for burial in Spynie Kirkyard beside those of his wife Margaret, who had died twenty-six years earlier.

The party welcoming Ramsay at Lossie station consists of Peter Smith 'Bo', later provost, and skipper of the *Succeed*, first steam drifter in Lossie, Provost Anderson, butcher, William Cormack, sailmaker, and Alexander Alexander, baker. The visitors include Lady Grant and Lord Thomson, one of Ramsay's closest political friends, who as Secretary of State for Air chose to travel on the fateful maiden voyage of the airship R101.

Ramsay was popular with his townsfolk and is seen here buying fish for his tea from Mrs Jessie Stewart, while his housekeeper, Miss McKenzie, delves in her purse for the money.

When he was re-elected as Prime Minister in 1929, Ramsay's car was pushed to the gate of the Hillocks by his friends. The car had been given to him by his friend Alexander Grant, originally a poor boy from Forres who by then owned McVitie and Price, biscuit manufacturers, when Grant discovered that the Prime Minister was neither provided with one nor able to afford one. Ramsay included Grant in his first honours list and the Tory press had a field day with accusations of sleaze, despite Grant's proud record of charitable donations over a number of years.

During the correspondence regarding his eventual expulsion from the Moray Golf Club because of his pacifist views, Ramsay informed the club that 'the visit of any prominent Liberal or Radical to the Moray Golf Club has been resented by a certain section which has not concealed its offensiveness either in the Club House or on the course', and as he waits at the starter's box with his sons Malcolm and Alister in this picture he appears to be getting the cold shoulder. He would have been one of very few locals to be a member of the club at the time, the majority being visitors from Elgin, Edinburgh or London.

Ivy Cottage was the Moray Golf Club's earliest clubhouse, but the popularity of the game was such that in 1893 the grand new building in the centre of this picture was opened by Sir William Gordon Cumming, the superior for the outer half of the land on which the course lay. In 1900 the clubhouse was greatly enlarged to cope with the continuing boom in membership, particularly among the ladies, who were given their own room and locker room. William Christie of Elgin opened the Stotfield Hotel (left) in 1895. It originally had 14 bedrooms, but within ten years the number had been increased to seventy, and soon a second hotel, the Marine, was built, although this was rather less successful. The Big Greenie, the open area in the foreground, was covered with herring nets laid out to dry out at the end of each season. When it was converted into a putting and bowling green to cater for the expanding tourist industry, Branderburgh and Stotfield were at last linked together.

Miss Asquith, daughter of the Prime Minister, presenting the trophy to George Thomson, winner of the 1913 Moray Open. Little did she know that within a few days she would be rescuing her father from attack at the hands of two militant suffragettes, one thought to be Christabel Pankhurst, on the 17th green (now the 18th of the new course). Thomson and his father were Elgin pharmacists who won lasting local fame for their Cod Liver Oil Cream. The oil was extracted by Isaac Spencer and company at factories at the Seatown – the oily works – and Aberdeen harbour. The Thomsons' cream made the oil almost palatable, and the presence of rum and brandy in the emulsion possibly helped to raise its popularity. The boy and girl caddies, many barefoot, are seated on the bank on the right.

A sundial stands in front of the clubhouse as a memorial to Sgt Edwards VC and Capt. George Edwards DSO, both caddies in their youth, and this is the official group at the dedication ceremony. The boy in shorts in the front row is Sandy Edwards, named after his uncle, who went on to become captain of the club and provost of the town.

Alexander Edwards, a cooper, joined the Seaforth Highlanders in September 1914 and quickly rose to the rank of sergeant. In 1917, while attacking a German machine-gun emplacement, he showed such gallantry as he led his men that he was awarded the Victoria Cross, here being presented by King George V. He returned home a hero, and was presented with a gold watch and a purse containing War Bonds, but sadly was killed when he returned to the front in 1918.

STOTFIELD LOSSIEMOUTH.

88262

The rocks at the Hythe, which had been Stotfield's harbour, were recognised as being lead-bearing as early as 1773, but at the time the small quantity of metal yielded did not cover the costs of its extraction. A fresh shaft was dug in 1852 with similar results. Third time was still unlucky, and after a further two years of operation the shaft was filled in. The chimney was demolished in 1897, and virtually the last traces of the mine vanished with the construction of houses on the site of the works buildings. The shaft can still be seen, and is just visible at the bottom right-hand corner of the picture, with spoil from the mine to the left.

Holiday Scene at Hythe Bay, Lossiemouth.

As the nineteenth century ended, Lossie townsfolk were treated to the novel sight of people going to sea for fun in a series of regattas organised by the visitors. The tent would have probably been rented from William Cormack, sail maker, who continued the rental trade until his business was destroyed in a fire in 1949.

The large houses along the skyline were usually occupied for only half of the year by their owners or tenants, and brought many well-to-do people to the town, often with a retinue of servants in tow. The wooden bungalow was built by local artist David West RSW, who won a considerable following with his water-colours of seascapes, and designed a combined support and sandbox for the golf club, eventually known as the Tee-caddy, still in use today.

On the Sands, Lossiemouth.

Perched on a rocky headland a mile west of the town is the Covesea Lighthouse, built in 1844 by Alan Stevenson, uncle of the more famous Robert Louis Stevenson. Like all others in Britain, it is now automatic, but for many years the keepers would climb to the top and raise the weights which worked the clockwork mechanism, turning the lenses which are now in Lossie Museum. The posts were for the salmon fishers to drape their nets over.

COVESEA LIGHTHOUSE, LOSSIEMOUTH.

BEACON, COVESEA SKERRIES, LOSSIEMOUTH.

On the Halliman Skerries just opposite the lighthouse stands a cast iron beacon with a cross on top, warning of the dangerous line of rocks scarcely visible at high tide. Its size can be gauged from the figure of local artist David West, posing on the steps having ventured out in his little sailboat.

The first Drainie Parish Kirk was built near Gordonstoun about 1676, and was replaced in 1823 by the one in the picture (left). This continued to be used until 1923 when it was dismantled to prevent it from falling into dereliction. A cottage on Coulardbank Farm was built from the stones, and the wood panelling was used to line the staircase in Gordonstoun; thus the fabric of the building was returned to the heritors whose responsibility it had been. The windows were incorporated into the house of David West but were lost in a fire a few years ago. James Ramsay MacDonald, the future Prime Minister, was a pupil and later a pupil-teacher at the parish school which was built alongside the church.

Drainie Church, Lossiemouth. J. D. Yeadon, Elgin.

Drainie Kirk was built to serve a parish consisting largely of farmers and their workers. As Lossie grew in size, the population of 1,000 in the 1821 census became 1,800 in 1851, and 3,497 in 1881. In 1849 the townspeople were given the convenience of a Chapel of Ease in the Elgin Road, saving them the long trek out to Drainie. Many years and much argument followed as they tried to get the Parish Kirk moved to the town, very much against the wishes of the farm folk. For a number of years the Chapel (right) was to provide the focus for worship in the town, but as the numbers and quality of the summer visitors increased it was eventually thought insufficiently grand for its purpose. When a new church was built at the head of the hill, it was abandoned, serving as a mortuary during the war, and eventually the Scout Hall before being demolished in favour of housing.

Most of the fishermen who had flocked to Lossie from 'doon the coast' had been Seceders, who had left the main stream of the Church of Scotland on the question of who should appoint the minister. They could not accept the right of the heritors – the landowners who were expected to build and maintain the building – to name the minister as a consequence. The first St James's was built in Street B (which eventually became Church Street), but it collapsed, and was replaced by the building now known as the Drill Hall because of its association for many years with the Territorial Army. A new church (above) was built in 1881 at a cost of £2,020 in James Street, James Square, although in this case the James was the Laird. The building was demolished in 1966 when the congregation moved to the empty High Church in Prospect Terrace, and the only features that have survived are the decorative pillars which stand on either side of the garage which replaced it.

In 1937 Carrie's beautiful shop (see page 2) and the Beatrice gown shop next door were completely gutted by fire, despite the best efforts of the local fire brigade, who did manage to prevent a large tank of paraffin in the back shop from exploding. The site had seen a fire some thirty years earlier, which probably accounts for the brick dividing wall, most unusual in the town.

In common with most Scottish towns, Lossie had its cafes run by Italian immigrants. It was a surprising fact that most such immigrants had no previous catering experience and were generally peasant farmers, mainly from the Cassino area between Rome and Naples, who had been driven from the land by poverty. Domenico Rizza arrived in Scotland in 1907, eventually taking over the Clifton Road shop which had been converted from a butchers shop into a cafe and billiard saloon by Luigi Zaccharini. Dom soon became one of Lossie's favourite characters, dispensing with a quiet smile excellent ice-cream in summer and hot drinks in winter. Oxo with lashings of pepper was a particular favourite in the thirties, and generations of boys listened to Raymond Glendenning broadcasting commentaries of the Scotland v England internationals on Dom's radio in the back room.

Almost all of the houses in Lossie and Branderburgh were built of local sandstone, and this gang is working in the last of the quarries, which closed in the 1950s. At the back are J. Cameron, A. Whyte, Davie Youngson and Alan Flood jnr., while the carter Nick Anderson holds his horse beside H. Alexander, Jock Flood, Wm. Ellis, Alan Flood sr., J. Stewart 'Wanner', and G. McCulloch. Jock's son Jackie survived jumping into the 50 foot deep quarry for a schoolboy dare with only a broken leg, but he was to die in 1945 along with his mother and four brothers when a Wellington bomber crashed on their house one Sunday morning, two weeks after VE Day. Only Jock and his daughter Jeannie survived.

One of the great agricultural advances at the end of the eighteenth century was the discovery that properly controlled drainage could greatly improve the productivity of land. A pocket of clay halfway between Lossie and Spynie provided the raw material for the Morayshire Tile Works, which as well as making drainage pipes also turned out bricks, replacing an earlier brickworks at Salterhill. The men cycled from Lossie or Elgin or else walked up the railway line to work. The works closed in the 1930s and the large chimney was demolished at the start of the war, being considered hazardous to the many aeroplanes by then flying 'circuits and bumps' from Lossie's aerodrome.

Between 1890 and 1945 two doctors, Thomas Brander and Robert Clark, provided medical care to Lossie. They were ably supported for 35 years by Queen's Nurse Mary Kelly, whose years of retirement were spent in a bungalow built in Dunbar Street for her by her grateful patients. Dr Brander's life almost ended when he fell into the Spey as a boy, and he was only saved by the salmon nets at its mouth. During the war, when the siren sounded, he had to run to the school to await casualties, and in 1942 declared four of his near neighbours dead, not knowing whether his wife was safe. In later years, after he suffered a heart attack, Mrs Brander drove her husband to visit his patients in a little Austin Seven, waiting outside wrapped in travelling rugs and with a hot water bottle for comfort. Their house, Craigmount, had been built by Alexander Cowie 'Billen', a fish merchant, who lost it when one herring season failed to produce herring he had already sold. We now call this dealing in futures, but it was standard practice many years ago.

Barking the Nets at Lossiemouth.

Herring nets only needed to be made of light cotton since they simply drifted in the water, waiting for the herring to swim into them as they fed. In order to prevent the nets from decaying, however, they were soaked in preservative made by dissolving the processed bark of the *acacia catecha* in hot water. The process was known as barking, and had a characteristic smell that was highly memorable. The nets became less pliable with each treatment, so that they were eventually discarded. Great attention was paid to drying the nets at every opportunity because the ownership of a net entitled a crew member to a share of the profits, if there were any, at the end of each season.

This happy group in a fine field of barley is 'bringing in the sheaves' after a good summer. When this picture was taken in 1931 most farm work was still manual and backbreaking, and the tractor would have been uncommon. Farm servants were tied or feed to the farm for six or twelve months for a set fee, with a cottage for the married men, or a bed in a 'chaumer' or bothy for the single ones. Farm labourers were a different category, working for a wage by the day or week, and probably living in the town.

When James Edwards married Annie Smith in 1878, they had already lived through the Indian Mutiny and the American Civil War. They were to live through the Boer War and the Great War before celebrating their golden wedding anniversary just before World War II broke out. Most houses in Branderburgh had the iron range seen in the picture, black leaded with Zebo and lovingly polished, as was the brass rail for airing clothes. James would have filled his pipe with XXX Bogie Roll, a thick twist of pungent tobacco which was cut into shreds in the smoker's palm using his Nest knife – no other brand would do for fishermen. James's boots were of the relatively fine leather favoured by the fishermen. Farm workers always wore boots of almost rigid leather, so that it was impossible to mistake the one for the other as they walked along the street.

Few families were unaffected by the Great War, and the whole town seems to have turned out at the War Memorial to the Fallen on the occasion of its unveiling by Capt. James Brander Dunbar in August 1922. Captain Dunbar had been twice wounded while serving with the Cameron Highlanders. The memorial was built into the rock face near the site of St Gerardine's cave, and bears the names of 35 sailors and 126 soldiers. This photograph was taken from a window in the station building, and the first name on the tablet added for the Second World War was that of James Birnie, son of the stationmaster. It seems strange to observe that all men wore caps or hats, the fashion now having changed.

Between the wars many men entered the reserve forces, the fishers joining the Naval Reserve and the landsmen the Territorials. The main reason they enrolled was because of the fortnight's camp each year – the nearest most got to a holiday in their lives. In 1939 the Reserves were called to the colours, and this group is about to board the train, being seen off by relatives and friends. The war was expected to be over by Christmas. The men are, at the back: Sye McKenzie, Alec Stewart 'Maglen' and Eddie Souter. In the front: Benj Souter, Isaac Ralph, Dod Cowie, 'Ailee' Mitchell, James Souter 'Soupee', Robbie Smith, Alexander 'Sye' Souter, John Crockett, Doddie Crockett, Doddie Mitchell, Jimmy Stewart 'Dairlie', John Stewart 'Candy', Alexander Stewart 'Colonel' and George Stewart 'Bowie'. Within a year, Soupee and Doddie Crockett were dead, the first killed while attempting to recover an enemy magnetic mine for examination, the second when his trawler hit a mine while returning from patrol off Portsmouth. A further six sailors were to die in 1940. Nineteen died in total, along with sixteen merchant seamen.

Having made their fortunes buying oranges and lemons in Lisbon and selling them in London, brothers James and Alexander Brander returned to Moray, and in 1765 bought the estate of Pitgaveny. This included the Loch of Spynie, trapped when the stony bank was thrown up at Lossiemouth. When they drained this into the river at Kays Brig (now Caysbriggs), a dispute arose over the ownership of the many acres of land that were uncovered. This led to a long and costly court case with Sir William Gordon of Gordonstoun, with the Branders winning, along with the Edinburgh lawyers. James's grandson, also James and a veteran of Waterloo, had the vision to see that a harbour could be constructed by cutting into the deserted rocky headland between the river mouth and Stotfield village, and was the first chairman of the Stotfield and Lossiemouth Harbour Company (as distinct from the Elgin and Lossiemouth Harbour Company which owned the river port). His nephew, Captain James Dunbar Brander, is the elderly gentleman in the chair, with his son Captain James Brander Dunbar at his shoulder.

The latter was to become the origin of John Buchan's *John MacNab* and the hero or villain of many stories about 'the Lairdie' over the 67 years he held the title. He enjoyed nothing better than winding up Lossie Town Council whenever he felt they were getting above themselves, and the Square was the focus of their disagreements on several occasions. Finally, in order to show whose Square it was, he sent a man to plough it, and although the plough broke on the rocky ground the point was made. For good measure he announced that he was to be buried in the Square opposite Provost Cormack's house, and kept a coffin in readiness for the rest of his long life. On the extreme right of the picture is Black Bob Geddes, head keeper and the scourge of Lossie poachers, beside 'Massa' who is thought to have returned with the Lairdie from his African adventures with Cecil Rhodes.

Not all of the parish lived conventional lives and several caves at Covesea and the lighthouse were homes to itinerant pedlars, in this case the Lindsays, with another cave occupied by a family of Campbells. A religious family known as 'the Joyfuls' were the last residents, about the time of the Great War.

This picture, entitled 'Covesea Cabin' shows another makeshift dwelling at Covesea, but this time above ground.

The days of the sailboats meant a great deal of employment for sailmakers, and John Alexander and his horse are waiting to take a sail from the loft to the boat skippered by James Mitchell on the right. In the cart Jock Cormack is ready for Peter Stewart 'Pom', unknown, Robert Cormack and Andrew Cowe to pass down the sail. This building was destroyed in a disastrous fire in 1949, when an assistant in the chandlers below knocked over a paraffin stove.

For many years from 1853 onwards, Lossie toyed with the idea of building a gasworks, but a final decision was always put off In 1913 it was decided to go for electricity instead, and in July 1914 the new generating station opened. This housed two engines of 55 hp, each driving a dynamo of 25 kW connected to a series of 125 large lead-acid accumulators. Ironically a small gas plant was needed to drive the engines until they were replaced by semi-diesels. Initially the charge was ten shillings per 33 watt lamp per annum. The manager, Bob Traill, was a man dedicated to serving the town and promoting the use of electricity. An exhibition in 1933 was so successful in promoting electricity for cooking that people could hardly get their tatties boiled on a Sunday when they all came out of church at the same time, and a connection to the Grampian electricity scheme at Elgin had to be negotiated. This had to be rectified, as Lossie remained on direct current until the arrival of the Hydro Board in 1948. The plates of the accumulators were separated by glass tubing, and at each cleaning of the tanks these were eagerly seized by boys for use as peashooters or 'spooties', used to propel elderberries for a short season before the spooties met their inevitable fate. The picture shows James Souter adjusting the voltage at the control board from which the entire supply system was run.

SO 2524 was an Elginshire registered Albion bus built in Scotstoun, Glasgow. It was supplied to Elgin and District Omnibus Co. in 1926, and ran on services between Elgin, Lossie and Stotfield. The frequency and timing of the bus service to Elgin was to occupy many hours in town council meetings for years to come, with particular concern that double deckers would fall over when turning from Pitgaveny Street into Queen Street. It never happened, although the manoeuvre was always exciting for the passengers.